<u>Disclaimer</u>

The content of "Modernization and its effects" is intended for informational and educational purposes only. The views and opinions expressed in this book are those of the author and do not necessarily reflect the official policy or position of any organization, institution, or individual.

While the author has made every effort to ensure the accuracy of the information presented, there may be errors or omissions. Readers are encouraged to conduct their own research and consult professionals in relevant fields when considering the implications of modernization.

The author and publisher are not responsible for any consequences arising from the use or misuse of the information contained in this book.

Foreword

In today's rapidly changing India, the idea of modernization can stir a mix of feelings such as excitement, uncertainty, and even resistance.

As our society grapples with the clash between cherished traditions and contemporary influences, it becomes increasingly important to explore how these changes shape our relationships, values, and identities. "Modernization and Its Effects" takes a deep dive into these complex dynamics, shedding light on the cultural shifts that define our lives.

This book examines how love and partnership are evolving, particularly among younger generations who are eager to redefine what family and commitment mean.

It looks at how technology influences our connections, the differences between urban and rural experiences, and the changing roles of gender in modern relationships.

By engaging with these themes, the book invites us to reflect on our own lives and the ways in which modernization impacts our choices.

What stands out in this exploration is the resilience of Indian society. While traditions remain significant, there is a palpable shift in attitudes, especially among the youth, who often find themselves balancing respect for their heritage with a desire for personal freedom and fulfillment.

This book captures that delicate dance beautifully, offering insights that resonate not just in India but also in many parts of the world facing similar transformations.

As you read through these pages, I encourage you to approach them with an open heart and mind. Consider how these themes resonate with your own experiences, and let them spark conversations in your community.

The journey toward understanding modernization is ongoing, and each of us plays a role in shaping a more inclusive future—one that honors our past while embracing new possibilities.

I am excited for you to explore the rich insights within this book, and I hope it inspires you to engage thoughtfully with the evolving narrative of modern relationships.

- Sai Surya Indraganti.

Preface

Writing "Modernization and Its Effects" has been a deeply personal journey for me. Growing up in India, I've seen firsthand how rapidly our society is changing. The vibrant tapestry of our traditions often feels at odds with the new influences of modern life, and this tension is something I've grappled with for years. This book is my attempt to explore those changes and share insights into how they shape our relationships, identities, and values.

My motivation to write came from a desire to understand the nuances of modernization and its impact on everyday life. I wanted to capture the stories of people navigating love, family, and societal expectations in a world that feels both exciting and overwhelming. As we strive for progress, we also confront challenges that require us to rethink long-held beliefs and adapt to new realities.

In these pages, you'll find discussions on various themes, including the balance between tradition and modernity, the role of technology in our lives, and the evolving identities of men and women in contemporary society.

I've aimed to highlight the rich diversity of experiences across different regions of India, recognizing that modernization affects us all in unique ways.

My hope is that this book serves as a conversation starter like the one that encourages you to reflect on your own experiences and engage with the complexities of modern life.

I believe that understanding these dynamics can foster empathy and promote meaningful discussions about how we can navigate our evolving society together.

I'm grateful to everyone who shared their stories with me and to those whose work inspired my thinking. Your voices have made this book richer and more relatable.

Thank you for being part of this journey. I hope you find the insights within these pages resonate with you and encourage you to think critically about the world we're building together.

- Sai Surya Indraganti.

Introduction

Overview of Modernization

Modernization is a term that evokes a lot of imagery and ideas. At its essence, it refers to the shift from traditional ways of living to more contemporary ones. This transformation touches almost every aspect of society such as: how we work, interact, and even think about our identities.

A Bit of History

To understand modernization, it helps to look back at the Industrial Revolution in the late 18th and early 19th centuries. This period marked a major turning point as societies moved from small, home-based production to large factories.

With this shift came urbanization, as people flocked to cities for work. In India, this journey has been shaped by a complex history that includes colonial rule and a quest for independence. Since then, modernization has been seen as a key to economic growth and social progress, but it hasn't been a straightforward path. Traditional structures often push back against change, creating a dynamic clash between the old and the new.

Key Aspects of Modernization

1. Economic Changes:

Modernization typically means a transition from farming to industrial and service-based economies. This shift can lead to greater productivity and new lifestyles focused on consumption.

2. Social Transformations:

As societies modernize, social roles often change. Traditional hierarchies may dissolve, leading to new ways of organizing communities. This is particularly true for gender roles, which are evolving rapidly in modern India.

3. Cultural Evolution:

Modernization can alter cultural practices and values. While globalization introduces fresh ideas and influences, it can also challenge and reshape local traditions.

4. Technological Progress:

The impact of technology is perhaps the most striking aspect of modernization. The digital age has transformed how we communicate and access information. In India, mobile technology and the internet are reshaping industries and personal relationships.

5. Political Changes:

Modernization often goes hand-in-hand with shifts in governance. As people demand more representation and rights, the political landscape evolves to meet these needs.

Purpose of the Book

"Modernization and Its Effects" seeks to unpack the various ways modernization impacts Indian society. Our focus will be on cultural differences, lifestyle changes, evolving work styles, and pressing social issues like toxicity in relationships, gender dynamics, and economic disparities.

Understanding India Today

In the context of India, modernization is a fascinating and often messy journey. With its rich tapestry of languages, religions, and cultures, the country offers a unique perspective on how modernization unfolds. This book aims to shed light on the differing impacts across urban and rural areas, recognizing that experiences can vary widely.

Cultural Dynamics

One key goal of this book is to delve into the cultural dynamics at play. While globalization fosters a flow of ideas, it can also lead to the dilution of traditional values.

Through personal stories and real-life examples, we'll explore the ongoing negotiations between embracing modernity and preserving cultural heritage.

Lifestyle Changes

As modernization sweeps through India, lifestyle shifts are inevitable. Urbanization has transformed everything from dietary habits to family structures. We'll analyze these changes, highlighting both the benefits and the challenges that come with adopting a modern lifestyle, including the rise of consumer culture.

Gender Dynamics

A significant theme will be the evolving role of gender in society. Feminism is gaining traction, challenging long-held patriarchal norms. However, issues like the misuse of women's rights have sparked intense debates. We'll explore these complexities, aiming for a nuanced understanding of the advancements and ongoing struggles in gender equality.

Wealth Management and Economic Disparities

As India integrates into the global economy, questions about wealth management and economic inequality become increasingly important. This book will address how modernization influences wealth distribution, financial literacy, and opportunities, especially for marginalized communities.

Modern Relationships and Marriages

Finally, we'll look at how modernization has transformed relationships and marriages. The shift from arranged marriages to love marriages, the influence of technology on dating, and changing expectations in partnerships will be explored. These dynamics illustrate the tension between traditional values and modern realities.

In summary, "Modernization and Its Effects" aims to provide a comprehensive exploration of how modernization shapes various aspects of life in India. By examining cultural differences, lifestyle changes, gender dynamics, economic issues, and evolving relationships, this book hopes to contribute to a deeper understanding of the complexities of modernization. As we navigate these transformative times, engaging critically with these topics will help us find more inclusive and equitable paths forward.

Topic 1

Cultural Differences in Modern India

Tradition vs. Modernity

The relationship between tradition and modernity in India is a complex and often contentious one. For centuries, India has been a land of rich cultural heritage, deeply rooted in customs, rituals, and social structures.

However, as modernization sweeps across the country, these traditional values are increasingly challenged. The tension between preserving age-old customs and embracing new ways of living is felt across various facets of life, from family dynamics to community interactions.

Cultural Heritage and Identity

At the heart of this tension lies India's diverse cultural heritage, which varies significantly from one region to another. Traditional Indian values often emphasize collectivism, familial ties, and respect for elders.

For instance, many communities still adhere to arranged marriages, where families play a pivotal role in partner selection. This practice is steeped in cultural beliefs that prioritize family reputation and social harmony over individual choice.

On the other hand, modern influences fueled by globalization, technology, and urbanization promote individualism, self-expression, and personal choice.

Young people today are more exposed to global trends through social media, which can lead to a clash with traditional norms.

For example, the rise of dating apps has shifted the dating landscape, challenging the very foundations of arranged marriages. The youth often grapple with the desire to honor their cultural heritage while also seeking the freedom to make personal choices.

Intergenerational Conflicts

This clash is particularly evident in intergenerational relationships. Older generations may feel threatened by the changing values of the youth, perceiving them as a departure from cultural norms.

In many families, this creates a rift where traditional values are upheld by parents and grandparents, while children lean towards modern ideals.

Discussions around marriage, career choices, and lifestyle preferences often spark intense debates, leading to feelings of frustration and misunderstanding on both sides.

Regional Variations

India's vastness and diversity mean that modernization does not affect all regions uniformly.

Different communities experience modernization in unique ways, influenced by local customs, economic opportunities, and levels of urbanization.

Urban vs. Rural Dynamics

In urban areas, the pace of modernization tends to be faster, with greater access to education, technology, and global cultural influences. Cities like Hyderabad, Mumbai and Bengaluru are melting pots of diverse cultures, where traditional values often coexist with modern lifestyles.

Here, young people are more likely to pursue higher education and career opportunities, which can lead to delayed marriages and a shift in family structures.

Conversely, rural communities often hold on to traditional values more firmly. While modernization is gradually making inroads, through improved infrastructure, education, and communication, many rural areas still prioritize customs and social structures that have been in place for generations.

For instance, the caste system remains a significant influence in many villages, shaping social interactions and marriage practices.

Economic Factors

Economic opportunities also play a crucial role in how different regions respond to modernization. In states like Punjab and Haryana, agricultural advancements and economic growth have led to changes in family structures and gender roles.

Women are increasingly taking on roles outside the home, contributing to household income and challenging traditional gender norms. However, this is often accompanied by a push-and-pull dynamic, where women face both empowerment and backlash within their communities.

In contrast, in more economically disadvantaged regions, such as parts of Bihar or Uttar Pradesh, traditional practices may be more resilient. Here, limited access to education and economic opportunities can reinforce traditional roles, especially for women. This highlights how modernization is not merely a linear process but it is shaped by local contexts, leading to different outcomes.

Case Studies: Cultural Shifts in Urban vs. Rural Settings

To illustrate these dynamics, we can explore specific case studies that highlight the cultural shifts occurring in urban and rural settings.

Case Study 1: The Urban Experience in Bengaluru

Bengaluru, known as the Silicon Valley of India, is a prime example of urban modernization. The city has attracted a young, tech-savvy population, leading to a vibrant culture that blends traditional values with modern influences. Here, young professionals often live independently, with many choosing to delay marriage in favor of career advancement.

A notable cultural shift can be seen in the approach to relationships. Dating apps have gained immense popularity, with many young people opting for casual dating rather than traditional courtship.

This shift has led to a redefinition of relationships, where individual preferences take precedence over familial expectations.

However, this urban lifestyle is not without its challenges. Many young individuals face societal pressures and familial expectations that clash with their modern choices. The tension often leads to a balancing act between embracing modernity and respecting traditional family values.

Case Study 2: The Rural Experience in Rajasthan

In contrast, Rajasthan, with its rich history and cultural heritage, provides a different lens through which to examine modernization. While urban centers in the state are experiencing change, many rural communities remain deeply rooted in tradition.

Here, arranged marriages are still the norm, and family reputation plays a crucial role in social interactions.

However, modernization is gradually making its presence felt. For instance, initiatives promoting education for girls have gained traction, leading to a slow but steady shift in gender roles.

More families are recognizing the importance of female education, allowing young women to pursue careers and become financially independent. This shift challenges traditional norms but is often met with resistance from conservative elements within the community.

Additionally, economic development in certain areas has led to increased mobility, with young people migrating to cities for better opportunities.

This migration can create cultural dislocation, as those who return home may bring different values and perspectives, further challenging traditional norms.

Case Study 3: The Middle Ground in Pune

Pune represents a middle ground, where urban and rural influences intertwine. This city has a rich educational environment and is home to many young professionals.

Here, the transition to modernity is evident, but traditional values remain influential.

In Pune, young people often experience a blend of modern and traditional lifestyles. For example, while many opt for love marriages, they still seek parental approval and consider familial expectations.

This hybrid approach reflects the ongoing negotiation between tradition and modernity, showcasing how individuals can adapt to changing times while honoring their cultural roots.

In conclusion, the cultural landscape of modern India is characterized by a dynamic interplay between tradition and modernity. As individuals and communities navigate this landscape, they face unique challenges and opportunities.

The tension between preserving cultural heritage and embracing modern influences is a defining feature of contemporary Indian society. By exploring regional variations and specific case studies, we gain valuable insights into how modernization shapes cultural identities across the country. This ongoing dialogue between the old and the new will continue to define India's cultural evolution in the years to come.

Topic 2
Changes in Lifestyle

The lifestyle of modern India is undergoing a seismic shift, influenced by a confluence of globalization, technological advancements, and urbanization.

As traditional practices give way to contemporary habits, the implications for daily life, social structures, and cultural practices are profound.

In this topic let's delve into how modernization has reshaped lifestyles across India, focusing on health and wellness trends, consumer behavior, family dynamics, and social interactions, highlighting both opportunities and challenges.

The Impact of Urbanization

Urbanization is one of the most significant aspects of modernization in India, transforming the way people live, work, and interact.

As millions flock to cities seeking better economic opportunities, the urban environment influences their values and behaviors, often creating a stark contrast with rural traditions.

Changing Living Conditions

In major cities like Hyderabad, Mumbai, Delhi, and Bengaluru, rapid urbanization has led to a reconfiguration of living conditions. High-rise apartments and gated communities have replaced sprawling family homes, pushing many families into smaller living spaces.

The trend toward living alone or in nuclear family units reflects a growing desire for independence among young adults.

For instance, a study of Bengaluru's demographics shows that many young professionals, particularly those in the tech industry, choose to live alone or with friends, often prioritizing location and affordability over space.

This shift impacts social relationships, as the traditional joint family system becomes less common. While this independence fosters personal growth, it can also lead to feelings of isolation, especially for those who miss the support networks that extended families provide.

Health and Wellness Trends

With urban living comes a transformation in health and wellness practices. Traditional diets, often centered on home-cooked meals rich in local ingredients, are increasingly being replaced by fast food and processed options.

The fast-paced nature of city life, with its long working hours and commutes, leaves little time for cooking or preparing healthy meals. Consequently, urban populations are witnessing a rise in lifestyle-related health issues, including obesity, hypertension, and diabetes.

However, this urbanization has also catalyzed a health and wellness movement. Fitness centers, yoga studios, and wellness retreats are flourishing, as individuals seek to reclaim their health amidst the chaos of urban life.

The rise of fitness influencers on social media platforms has further propelled this trend, encouraging a younger generation to adopt healthier lifestyles. Many urbanites now prioritize fitness and well-being, participating in marathons, yoga classes, and nutrition workshops, blending modern fitness trends with traditional practices like yoga and Ayurveda.

Consumer Culture

As India embraces modernization, consumer culture has become a defining characteristic of contemporary life.

With rising disposable incomes and exposure to global brands, the way people perceive and engage in consumption is undergoing a significant transformation.

The Rise of the Middle Class

The expansion of the middle class in India has been a major driver of this consumerist wave. With access to better education and job opportunities, families are spending more on leisure, travel, and lifestyle choices.

The aspiration for a higher quality of life is leading to increased consumption across various sectors, including technology, fashion, and entertainment.

For example, the smartphone market in India has exploded, with brands catering specifically to Indian consumers, offering affordable yet feature-rich devices.

This accessibility to technology has reshaped how people communicate, work, and access information, creating a culture of constant connectivity and instant gratification.

e-Commerce and Changing Shopping Habits

The advent of e-commerce has revolutionized shopping habits, particularly among younger consumers.

Platforms like Flipkart and Amazon have made it possible to purchase goods from the comfort of home, drastically changing the retail landscape.

This shift has led to a decline in traditional marketplaces, although many are adapting by incorporating online sales channels.

The convenience of online shopping has influenced purchasing behaviors, with consumers now seeking instant access to products. Flash sales, discounts, and home delivery services have become key motivators for purchases, creating a culture where immediacy and convenience are paramount.

However, this trend also raises questions about sustainability, as the increase in consumption often leads to greater waste and environmental concerns.

Social Media Influence

Social media is another powerful force shaping consumer culture in modern India.

Platforms like Instagram, Facebook, and TikTok are not only venues for social interaction but also significant marketing tools. Influencers play a crucial role in driving trends, promoting products, and shaping consumer preferences.

The impact of social media on consumer behavior can be profound. Many young people find themselves navigating a landscape where online presence and brand affiliation dictate social status.

This culture of comparison can lead to financial strain, as individuals prioritize material possessions and lifestyle choices over savings and long-term investments.

The pressure to conform to social media ideals often results in a cycle of consumption that can be difficult to break.

Family Dynamics

The shifts in lifestyle brought about by modernization are also evident in family dynamics, where traditional roles and structures are evolving.

The once-dominant joint family system is increasingly giving way to nuclear families, with implications for relationships and responsibilities within households.

The Transition to Nuclear Families

The movement toward nuclear families signifies a cultural shift that reflects changing societal values. Young couples are opting to live independently, valuing privacy, autonomy, and a more egalitarian approach to relationships.

This evolution allows for a redistribution of household responsibilities, as partners share duties related to work and home life more equally.

However, this transition is not without challenges. Nuclear families may struggle with the absence of the support systems that extended families traditionally provided.

New parents, for example, often find themselves navigating the complexities of child-rearing without the guidance and assistance of grandparents or a broader family network.

This can lead to increased stress and feelings of isolation, especially for women who may bear the brunt of household responsibilities alongside their careers.

Changing Gender Roles

As modernization reshapes family dynamics, gender roles within households are also evolving. Women in urban areas are increasingly pursuing higher education and career opportunities, challenging long-standing societal expectations that prioritize homemaking.

This shift represents significant progress toward gender equality, as women assert their right to choose their paths.

However, the transition is often fraught with contradictions. While many women are gaining independence, they frequently face the dual burden of managing careers and household duties.

The expectation to excel in both realms can lead to stress and burnout, raising important questions about work-life balance and the equitable distribution of responsibilities within the family.

Social Interactions and Community Life

As lifestyles change, so too do social interactions and community life. The urban environment fosters new forms of connection, while traditional community bonds in rural areas are being tested by modernization.

Technology's Role in Relationships

Technology has transformed social interactions, facilitating communication across distances while simultaneously affecting the depth of personal connections.

Social media platforms allow individuals to stay in touch with friends and family, but they can also foster a superficial sense of community. In many cases, face-to-face interactions are being replaced by online conversations, leading to concerns about genuine connection and emotional intimacy.

The rise of online dating apps reflects this shift. While they provide new avenues for meeting partners, they also introduce challenges related to commitment and communication.

Many young people find themselves caught in a cycle of casual relationships, where the focus on instant gratification can hinder the development of deeper, meaningful connections.

Community Engagement in Rural Areas

In contrast, rural communities maintain a strong sense of social cohesion, rooted in traditions that emphasize community involvement. Festivals, local gatherings, and communal events remain integral to social life, fostering relationships built on shared experiences and collective identity.

However, even in these settings, modernization is starting to alter the fabric of community life. Migration to urban areas for work is common, leading to demographic shifts that can weaken traditional ties. Younger generations, drawn by the allure of city life, may find themselves less engaged with their roots, impacting the transmission of cultural practices and values.

The Role of Education and Awareness

Education plays a vital role in shaping modern lifestyles, particularly in how young people approach relationships, health, and consumption. As access to education improves, individuals become more aware of global issues such as sustainability, health, and gender equality. This increased awareness can lead to shifts in behavior, with many young Indians advocating for social change and actively engaging in community initiatives.

For instance, awareness campaigns around issues like gender violence, mental health, and environmental sustainability are gaining traction, driven by young activists who leverage social media to amplify their voices.

This engagement not only reflects changing lifestyles but also signals a growing commitment to addressing societal challenges.

In conclusion, the changes in lifestyle brought about by modernization are reshaping various aspects of life in India. Urbanization, consumer culture, evolving family dynamics, and changing social interactions highlight both the opportunities and challenges that accompany this transformation.

While modernization fosters independence, innovation, and greater awareness, it also raises critical questions about the sustainability of these changes and their impact on traditional values.

As India continues to navigate this complex landscape, understanding the implications of these lifestyle changes is crucial. The interplay between tradition and modernity will shape the future of Indian society, influencing everything from cultural practices to social structures.

In the subsequent topics, we will delve deeper into specific aspects of these changes, particularly focusing on gender dynamics and the socio-economic disparities that accompany modernization.

Topic 3: Working Styles

The working styles in modern India have undergone significant transformation in recent years, driven by globalization, technological advancements, and shifts in societal expectations. As the nation grapples with the complexities of a rapidly evolving economy, the nature of work itself is being redefined. This topic explores the changing landscape of work in India, examining workplace culture, the rise of remote work, gender dynamics, and the influence of technology on professional life.

Evolving Workplace Culture

From Traditional to Modern Workplaces

Historically, Indian workplaces were often characterized by hierarchical structures and a strong emphasis on seniority. Employees typically adhered to a formal dress code, and communication was often top-down, with little room for open dialogue. However, as the economy has expanded and globalized, a more dynamic and collaborative workplace culture has emerged.

In contemporary offices, especially in metropolitan areas, there is a noticeable shift toward flatter organizational structures. Companies are increasingly embracing a culture of openness, where ideas can flow freely across levels. This transformation is evident in sectors like technology, where startups are often at the forefront of fostering informal work environments that encourage creativity and innovation.

Diversity and Inclusion

Diversity and inclusion have become key focal points in modern workplaces. Organizations are recognizing the importance of building teams that reflect a variety of backgrounds, perspectives, and experiences. This shift not only enhances creativity and problem-solving but also aligns with global best practices in talent management.

Companies are implementing diversity training and initiatives aimed at creating inclusive environments where all employees feel valued. The rise of women in leadership roles and the increasing visibility of LGBTQ+ employees are indicative of this change, though challenges remain in fully achieving equity across all sectors.

The Rise of Remote Work

Impact of the Pandemic

The COVID-19 pandemic accelerated the adoption of remote work in India, transforming the traditional office landscape overnight. Prior to the pandemic, remote work was often viewed as a privilege, limited to certain roles or industries.

However, the necessity of maintaining business continuity during lockdowns forced organizations to adapt quickly.

As a result, many companies have now integrated flexible work arrangements into their policies.

Remote work has proven to be beneficial in several ways, including increased productivity and reduced commuting time. Employees appreciate the flexibility to create their own work environments, which often leads to improved work-life balance.

Challenges of Remote Work

Despite its advantages, remote work also presents unique challenges. Isolation can become a significant issue, as employees miss out on the social interactions and camaraderie that an office environment fosters. Furthermore, the blurring of boundaries between personal and professional life can lead to burnout, as the expectation to be available outside of traditional working hours increases.

Companies are responding to these challenges by fostering virtual team-building activities and investing in mental health resources. Regular check-ins and open communication channels have become essential for maintaining team cohesion and morale in a remote setting.

Gender Dynamics in the Workplace

Changing Roles and Expectations

Modernization has brought about significant changes in gender roles within the workplace. Traditionally, Indian women faced numerous barriers to career advancement, often relegated to supportive roles or excluded from leadership positions. However, as more women enter the workforce and pursue higher education, this dynamic is shifting.

The participation of women in the labor force has increased, particularly in sectors like IT, healthcare, and education. Women are not only taking on roles in entry-level positions but are also making strides in leadership and managerial roles. Initiatives aimed at supporting women's career advancement, such as mentorship programs and skill development workshops, are increasingly common.

Workplace Challenges

Despite these advancements, women continue to face significant challenges in the workplace. Gender bias and discrimination remain prevalent, often manifesting in pay disparities and limited opportunities for career growth.

Balancing work and family responsibilities is another critical issue, as women are still expected to manage household duties alongside their professional commitments.

Organizations are beginning to address these challenges by implementing policies that promote work-life balance, such as flexible working hours and parental leave.

However, societal expectations and traditional gender roles often complicate these efforts, making it essential for companies to cultivate a culture that genuinely supports gender equality.

The Influence of Technology

Technological Advancements and the Future of Work

Technology is transforming how work is conducted across all sectors. The rise of artificial intelligence, automation, and data analytics is reshaping job roles and responsibilities, requiring employees to adapt and acquire new skills continually. Industries that were once labor-intensive are now increasingly reliant on technology to enhance efficiency and productivity.

For example, in the manufacturing sector, robotics and automation are streamlining production processes, while in the financial sector, fintech solutions are revolutionizing traditional banking practices. This shift is creating demand for a workforce that is not only technologically savvy but also capable of critical thinking and problem-solving.

Continuous Learning and Upskilling

As technology continues to evolve, the importance of continuous learning and upskilling has become paramount. Professionals must remain competitive by investing in their education and staying abreast of industry trends. Online courses, webinars, and training programs have surged in popularity, allowing individuals to acquire new skills at their own pace.

Organizations are also recognizing the need for employee development and are investing in training programs to ensure their workforce remains adaptable. This focus on lifelong learning is fostering a culture of innovation, where employees are encouraged to experiment, take risks, and contribute creatively to their organizations.

Work-Life Balance and Employee Well-Being

The Search for Balance

As work styles evolve, the quest for work-life balance has become a prominent concern for many employees. The rise of remote work and flexible hours presents both opportunities and challenges in achieving this balance.

While employees appreciate the flexibility, the constant connectivity that technology affords can blur the lines between work and personal life.

Organizations are increasingly recognizing the importance of employee well-being and are implementing initiatives to support work-life balance.

Mental health resources, wellness programs, and flexible work arrangements are becoming standard offerings. Companies that prioritize employee well-being often see improved productivity and job satisfaction, fostering a more engaged and committed workforce.

Mental Health Awareness

The conversation around mental health in the workplace is gaining traction, particularly in the wake of the pandemic. Employees are increasingly voicing their concerns about stress, anxiety, and burnout, leading organizations to take proactive measures. Providing mental health resources, such as counseling services and stress management workshops, is becoming a priority for many companies.

This cultural shift towards prioritizing mental health reflects a broader societal change, as stigma surrounding mental health issues continues to diminish. Open discussions about mental well-being are paving the way for healthier workplaces, where employees feel empowered to seek help without fear of judgment.

The Future of Work in India

Hybrid Work Models

Looking ahead, hybrid work models that combine remote and in-office work are likely to become the norm. This approach allows for greater flexibility while also facilitating collaboration and relationship-building. Organizations will need to carefully consider how to structure their teams to maximize the benefits of both remote and in-person work.

As companies adopt hybrid models, they must also address the potential challenges that arise. Ensuring effective communication, fostering team cohesion, and providing equal opportunities for all employees, regardless of their work location, will be critical to success.

Embracing Change

The future of work in India will require a willingness to embrace change and adapt to new realities. As technology continues to evolve, employees must remain agile and open to learning. Organizations, in turn, will need to cultivate cultures that support innovation, collaboration, and diversity.

By fostering an environment that encourages continuous growth and adaptability, India can position itself as a leader in the global workforce, harnessing the potential of its diverse population to drive economic growth and social progress.

In summary, the working styles in modern India are undergoing significant transformation, shaped by evolving workplace cultures, the rise of remote work, changing gender dynamics, and the pervasive influence of technology.

While these changes present opportunities for innovation and growth, they also pose challenges that require careful consideration and proactive strategies.

As India navigates this complex landscape, understanding the implications of these working styles is crucial for individuals and organizations alike.

The future of work will demand a commitment to continuous learning, inclusivity, and employee well-being, ensuring that all individuals can thrive in an ever-changing environment.

In the following topics, we will explore the evolving dynamics of relationships and marriages in modern India, shedding light on how these shifts intersect with broader societal changes.

Topic 4: Increase of Toxicity in People

Introduction

In modern Indian society, the rise of toxic behavior is an increasingly pressing issue that warrants deep exploration. The factors contributing to this toxicity are multifaceted, encompassing societal pressures, economic disparities, and the pervasive influence of social media.

However, a significant underlying element is the impact of toxic parenting, unhealed childhood traumas, and unresolved emotional wounds from past relationships. Understanding these deeper layers is vital to address the toxicity that permeates personal relationships and community dynamics.

This topic delves into the nature of toxicity, its manifestations, and strategies for healing and fostering healthier interactions.

Defining Toxicity

Understanding Toxic Behavior

Toxicity in interpersonal relationships encompasses a range of harmful actions and attitudes that negatively affect others. These behaviors often include manipulation, emotional abuse, excessive criticism, and a lack of accountability.

Individuals who exhibit toxic traits may be unaware of their impact, perpetuating a cycle of negativity that affects everyone around them.

In the context of modern India, toxic behaviors are manifested in various settings such as families, workplaces, friendships, and online interactions. The fast-paced, competitive nature of contemporary life can exacerbate these tendencies, leading to environments where personal gain is prioritized over collective well-being.

Identifying Toxic Traits

Recognizing toxic traits is crucial for individuals seeking to protect their mental and emotional health. Common indicators include persistent negativity, manipulative behavior, gaslighting, and an inability to accept responsibility. Understanding these traits allows individuals to distance themselves from harmful relationships and seek healthier interactions.

The Role of Toxic Parenting

Understanding Toxic Parenting

Toxic parenting refers to behaviors that adversely affect a child's emotional and psychological development. This can manifest through emotional neglect, excessive control, criticism, or manipulation. In India, traditional family structures often emphasize obedience and respect for authority, which can lead to unhealthy dynamics.

For example, parents may impose unrealistic expectations on their children, leading to feelings of inadequacy. This pressure can create a toxic environment where children feel they must conform to rigid norms, stifling their individuality and self-worth.

The Impact on Children

Children raised in toxic environments often grapple with a range of emotional and behavioral issues. They may internalize negative beliefs about themselves, resulting in anxiety, depression, and difficulties forming healthy relationships. The lack of emotional support and validation can hinder their ability to develop a positive self-image.

As these children grow into adults, they may replicate toxic behaviors in their relationships. They might struggle with setting boundaries, often oscillating between enmeshment and detachment in their interactions, perpetuating a cycle of toxicity.

Breaking the Cycle of Toxic Parenting

Addressing toxic parenting requires awareness and a commitment to change. Parents must recognize their behaviors and understand their impact on their children. This awareness can lead to seeking therapy or counseling to explore healthier parenting strategies.

Open communication is essential in breaking this cycle. Encouraging children to express their feelings and opinions fosters a sense of autonomy and self-worth. By providing a supportive environment, parents can help cultivate emotional resilience in their children.

Unhealed Childhood Traumas

Understanding Childhood Trauma

Childhood trauma refers to adverse experiences that significantly disrupt a child's emotional and psychological development. These experiences can include physical, emotional, or sexual abuse, neglect, and exposure to domestic violence. In India, societal expectations and stigmas surrounding mental health can exacerbate the prevalence of childhood trauma.

Children who endure trauma may struggle with emotional regulation, self-esteem, and relationship dynamics in adulthood. The unresolved issues stemming from these experiences can persist, leading to challenges in forming healthy, trusting relationships.

Manifestations of Unhealed Trauma

Unhealed childhood trauma often manifests in adult relationships through trust issues, fear of intimacy, and heightened sensitivity to criticism. Individuals may engage in self-sabotaging behaviors, believing they are unworthy of love and support.

For instance, someone who experienced emotional neglect may struggle to trust their partner, leading to conflict and withdrawal. Conversely, individuals who faced emotional abuse may become overly defensive or critical, creating a toxic dynamic in their interactions.

Healing from Childhood Trauma

Addressing unhealed childhood trauma is essential for breaking the cycle of toxicity. Therapeutic approaches such as cognitive-behavioral therapy (CBT) and trauma-focused therapy can help individuals process their experiences and develop coping strategies.

Creating safe spaces for individuals to share their experiences is equally important. Support groups and community programs can provide resources and connections, allowing individuals to heal together and understand they are not alone in their struggles.

Unresolved Issues from Past Relationships

Understanding Past Relationship Trauma

Unresolved issues from past relationships can have a profound impact on current interactions. Emotional baggage carried from previous partnerships often leads to trust issues, fear of commitment, or heightened sensitivity to perceived slights. In a modern context, where relationships are frequently influenced by societal expectations, these issues can be intensified.

The end of a significant relationship can trigger feelings of failure or inadequacy, leading individuals to become hesitant to engage in new partnerships. The fear of repeating past mistakes can stifle emotional growth and connection.

Manifestations of Relationship Trauma

Unresolved relationship issues can manifest in various ways. Individuals may become overly critical or clingy, constantly seeking validation and reassurance from their partners. Alternatively, some may exhibit avoidance behaviors, distancing themselves emotionally to protect against potential hurt.

In romantic contexts, these unresolved issues create toxic dynamics. One partner may feel overwhelmed by the other's insecurities, while the other feels rejected, leading to misunderstandings and resentment.

Healing from Relationship Trauma

To heal from unresolved relationship issues, individuals must first acknowledge their feelings and experiences. Self-reflection and journaling can help them understand their patterns and triggers, enabling personal growth.

Therapy plays a critical role in addressing past relationship trauma. A therapist can assist individuals in processing their experiences, working through feelings of grief or loss, and developing healthier coping mechanisms.

Open communication with current partners is vital. Encouraging discussions about fears, insecurities, and expectations can help rebuild trust and create a supportive environment for healing.

The Interconnectedness of Toxicity

The Cycle of Toxicity

The interplay between toxic parenting, unhealed childhood traumas, and unresolved relationship issues creates a cycle of toxicity that can be challenging to break. Individuals who grow up in toxic environments are more likely to exhibit similar behaviors in their relationships, perpetuating a cycle of negativity.

For instance, a person raised by a toxic parent may enter adulthood with deep-seated insecurities, leading them to engage in toxic behaviors toward their partners. Conversely, unresolved relationship traumas can trigger defensive mechanisms that contribute to toxic dynamics.

Addressing Interconnected Issues

To effectively address toxicity, it is essential to recognize the interconnectedness of these issues. Individuals must explore their childhood experiences and relationship histories to gain insight into their current behaviors.

Programs that offer holistic approaches to healing can be particularly effective. By combining therapeutic practices with community support and educational resources, individuals can develop a comprehensive understanding of their emotional landscape and cultivate healthier patterns of interaction.

Fostering Healthy Relationships

Cultivating Emotional Intelligence

Emotional intelligence is critical for fostering healthy relationships and mitigating toxicity. Developing self-awareness and empathy allows individuals to navigate their emotions and understand the feelings of others more effectively.

Education programs focused on emotional intelligence can help individuals recognize and address toxic behaviors. Implementing these programs in schools, workplaces, and community organizations promotes healthy interpersonal dynamics.

Encouraging Open Communication

Open communication is vital for building trust and understanding in relationships. Encouraging individuals to express their feelings and concerns without fear of judgment creates a safe environment for growth.

Workshops and training sessions on effective communication skills can empower individuals to articulate their needs and expectations clearly. Practicing active listening and validating each other's experiences fosters a supportive atmosphere that encourages healing.

Creating Supportive Communities

Building supportive communities is essential for addressing toxicity. Support groups, workshops, and community events can provide individuals with the resources and connections they need to heal and grow.

By fostering environments that prioritize empathy, understanding, and respect, society can work toward reducing toxicity. Encouraging individuals to share their experiences and support one another creates a sense of belonging and resilience.

The Role of Education and Awareness

Raising Awareness

Education and awareness are crucial in combating toxicity. Schools, workplaces, and community organizations can implement programs focusing on social-emotional learning, conflict resolution, and effective communication skills. By equipping individuals with the tools to navigate relationships constructively, society can work towards reducing toxicity.

Public campaigns that raise awareness about mental health and the effects of toxic behavior can help destigmatize these issues. Encouraging open discussions about mental health fosters greater understanding and support within communities.

Empowering Individuals

Empowering individuals to prioritize their mental health and well-being is essential for combating toxicity. Providing access to mental health resources, counseling, and support groups can help individuals cope with their challenges.

Encouraging resilience and coping strategies empowers individuals to address toxic behaviors constructively. Teaching stress management techniques, mindfulness practices, and self-care strategies can equip individuals to handle toxic situations more effectively.

In conclusion, the increase of toxicity in modern India is a multifaceted issue influenced by various factors, including toxic parenting, unhealed childhood traumas, and unresolved relationship issues. Addressing these underlying issues is crucial for fostering healthier interactions and promoting overall well-being.

By recognizing the interconnectedness of these factors, individuals can take proactive steps toward healing and growth. Education, open communication, and community support are vital for mitigating toxicity and promoting emotional resilience.

As India navigates the complexities of modernization, understanding and addressing the roots of toxic behavior will be crucial for creating a healthier, more supportive society. The journey toward healing and positive change begins with awareness, empathy, and a commitment to fostering healthier relationships.

Topic 5

Misuse of Women's Rights and Evolving Concepts of Feminism, Patriarchy, and Misogyny

Introduction

The fight for women's rights in India has witnessed remarkable progress over the past few decades, yet it is marred by complex challenges that often obscure the achievements made. The advancement of women's rights has been accompanied by a troubling trend, which is the misuse of these rights. This misuse can create skepticism and backlash that complicates the genuine pursuit of gender equality. To understand this phenomenon, it's essential to explore the interplay between feminism, patriarchal structures, and misogyny within the contemporary Indian context. This topic delves into these dynamics, aiming to shed light on the current state of women's rights and the societal attitudes that shape them.

Understanding Women's Rights in India

Historical Context

To appreciate the current state of women's rights in India, we must first acknowledge their historical roots. Traditional Indian society has long confined women to roles that emphasize domesticity and subservience. However, the seeds of change were planted during the independence movement, where women actively participated alongside men in the struggle for freedom.

Figures such as Sarojini Naidu and Kamaladevi Chattopadhyay were not only advocates for their rights but also symbols of women's contributions to nation-building.

Following independence, the Indian Constitution was adopted, enshrining gender equality as a fundamental right. This marked a significant turning point, as various laws were enacted to safeguard women's rights. Despite these advancements, the challenge lies in the implementation of these laws within a society still grappling with deep-seated patriarchal norms.

Current Status of Women's Rights

Today, women in India have access to a myriad of rights concerning education, employment, and health. However, the reality is often starkly different from the legal framework.

Women frequently encounter numerous obstacles, including gender-based violence, workplace discrimination, and societal pressure to adhere to traditional gender roles.

Misuse of women's rights further complicates the landscape. Instances of false allegations or weaponization of legal protections can lead to widespread skepticism about genuine claims of abuse and harassment.

This phenomenon not only discredits authentic victims but also poses a significant threat to the integrity of the feminist movement.

The Misuse of Women's Rights

Understanding Misuse

The misuse of women's rights manifests in various forms, most notably through false accusations of harassment or domestic violence. Such misuse can undermine the credibility of legitimate claims, creating an atmosphere of doubt and suspicion. When high-profile cases arise where allegations are questioned, it can shift public perception and engender a narrative that women are misusing their rights.

This misuse has real-world consequences. Victims of genuine abuse may hesitate to come forward, fearing disbelief or repercussions from the very systems that are supposed to protect them. This creates a chilling effect, where the fear of false accusations looms large over discussions about women's rights.

Impact on Feminist Movements

The misuse of women's rights presents significant challenges for feminist movements. High-profile cases of alleged misuse can overshadow the struggles of women facing real violence and discrimination.

As a result, the feminist narrative can be co-opted, leading to perceptions that feminists are exaggerating issues or misusing their rights.

This dynamic has led to divisions within the feminist movement itself. Some activists advocate for a more cautious approach in discussing women's rights, while others argue that we must not shy away from robust advocacy for victims. This internal conflict highlights the need for a nuanced understanding of women's rights and the complexities of their implementation.

Addressing Misuse

To effectively combat the misuse of women's rights, fostering a culture of accountability is essential. This begins with education—raising awareness about both the importance of women's rights and the potential for misuse. Implementing programs that provide comprehensive training for law enforcement and legal professionals can ensure that cases are handled with sensitivity and thoroughness.

Additionally, creating robust support systems for genuine victims is crucial. Establishing confidential reporting mechanisms and safe spaces can encourage women to share their experiences without fear of judgment. Legal reforms that emphasize thorough investigations can also help restore faith in the systems designed to protect women.

Evolving Concepts of Feminism

Historical Feminism in India

The feminist movement in India has evolved through various phases, each marked by its unique focus. Early feminists were primarily concerned with securing basic rights such as education, the right to vote, and legal protection.

They sought to challenge societal norms that confined women to domestic roles and advocated for greater participation in public life.

In the decades following independence, the focus shifted to legal reforms aimed at protecting women's rights. Activists worked tirelessly to enact laws addressing dowry, domestic violence, and workplace harassment. The late 20th century saw the emergence of more radical feminist voices who began addressing issues like sexual autonomy and reproductive rights.

Contemporary Feminism

Today's feminism in India is diverse and multifaceted. It encompasses a broad range of issues, including intersectionality, LGBTQ+ rights, and environmental justice.

Contemporary feminists recognize that the struggles faced by women are not monolithic; rather, they are shaped by intersecting identities such as caste, class, religion, and sexuality.

Social media has become a powerful tool for contemporary feminism, amplifying voices and mobilizing action. Movements like #MeToo have highlighted the prevalence of sexual harassment and violence, encouraging women to share their experiences and seek accountability.

Challenges Within Feminism

Despite its progress, the feminist movement faces several challenges, including internal divisions and external backlash. The rise of counter-movements that oppose feminist ideologies has intensified scrutiny of women's rights advocates.

Misogynistic narratives often emerge in public discourse, framing feminists as extremists or portraying their demands as unreasonable.

Moreover, the commercialization of feminism poses risks to its authenticity. Corporations may adopt feminist rhetoric for marketing purposes without genuinely addressing the underlying issues.

This commodification can dilute the movement's message, reducing it to a trend rather than a profound societal change.

The Role of Patriarchy

Understanding Patriarchy

Patriarchy, the societal structure that privileges men and upholds traditional gender roles, continues to wield considerable influence in India. Patriarchal norms dictate expectations for both men and women, often reinforcing rigid stereotypes that limit personal freedoms.

In many communities, patriarchal attitudes manifest in various ways, from the expectation that women prioritize family over career to societal pressure for early marriage. These norms restrict women's opportunities and perpetuate systemic inequalities, making it difficult for them to assert their rights.

Patriarchy's Influence on Women's Rights

Patriarchal structures often undermine women's rights by perpetuating harmful stereotypes and limiting access to education and economic opportunities. Women may face discrimination in professional settings, encounter barriers to advancement, and experience harassment without adequate recourse.

Moreover, societal attitudes toward gender-based violence often reflect patriarchal values. Victims may be blamed for their circumstances, and abusive behavior may be excused or overlooked. This perpetuates a culture of silence around violence, further entrenching gender inequality.

Challenging Patriarchal Norms

Challenging patriarchal norms requires a concerted effort at multiple levels. Education plays a crucial role in reshaping attitudes and fostering a culture of equality.

Incorporating gender studies into school curricula can help children understand and question traditional roles.

Engaging men in conversations about gender equality is also essential. Initiatives that encourage men to advocate for women's rights can dismantle the stigma surrounding feminism and create allies in the struggle for equality.

The Impact of Misogyny

Understanding Misogyny

Misogyny, characterized by the hatred of women, is a pervasive issue that intertwines with patriarchy and the misuse of women's rights. This deeply ingrained attitude manifests in various forms, including discrimination, objectification, and violence against women.

In India, cultural narratives often depict women in limiting roles, tying their worth to their relationships with men—be it as mothers, wives, or daughters. Such objectification reinforces gender inequalities and fosters a climate where misogynistic attitudes thrive.

Consequences of Misogyny

The consequences of misogyny are far-reaching, impacting women's mental and physical health. Women who face misogynistic attitudes may experience anxiety, depression, and a diminished sense of self-worth. This climate of fear and oppression stifles their potential and limits their opportunities.

Moreover, misogyny normalizes violence against women, creating a society where abusive behavior is often tolerated or dismissed.

This normalization perpetuates gender inequality and hinders efforts to promote women's rights.

Addressing Misogyny

Combating misogyny requires a multi-pronged approach that includes education, advocacy, and media representation. Educational programs that challenge stereotypes and promote gender equality can help shift societal attitudes.

Media plays a powerful role in shaping perceptions of women. Promoting diverse and empowering portrayals of women in films, television, and advertising can counteract misogynistic narratives and foster a more equitable society.

The Way Forward

Empowering Women

Empowering women is critical for fostering a society that values equality and justice. Initiatives that focus on education, economic independence, and leadership opportunities can help women reclaim their rights and challenge societal norms.

Support networks and mentorship programs can provide women with resources and guidance, allowing them to navigate personal and professional challenges effectively. Encouraging women to engage in advocacy and activism amplifies their voices and influence in the public sphere.

Fostering Inclusive Feminism

Creating a more inclusive feminist movement involves recognizing and addressing the diverse experiences of women across different backgrounds. Intersectionality should serve as a guiding principle, acknowledging how caste, class, religion, and sexuality intersect to shape women's lives.

Engaging in dialogue that promotes understanding and solidarity among various feminist groups can strengthen the movement. This collaborative approach allows for a more comprehensive understanding of the challenges women face and the solutions needed to address them.

Promoting Gender Sensitivity

Promoting gender sensitivity across all sectors of society is vital for creating lasting change. Training programs for educators, employers, and community leaders can foster a culture of respect and inclusivity.

Encouraging men to take an active role in advocating for gender equality can challenge patriarchal norms. Collaborative efforts between genders can dismantle harmful stereotypes and create a more equitable society.

In conclusion, the dynamics surrounding women's rights in modern India are intricate and multifaceted.

While significant progress has been made, challenges persist, particularly concerning the misuse of rights, the influence of patriarchy, and the prevalence of misogyny.

Addressing these issues requires a holistic approach that encompasses education, advocacy, and community engagement.

By fostering an inclusive feminist movement that embraces the diverse experiences of women, society can work toward dismantling the structures that perpetuate inequality.

Empowering women, promoting gender sensitivity, and challenging patriarchal norms are essential steps in creating a more equitable and just society.

As India navigates the complexities of modernization, understanding and addressing the interplay of women's rights, feminism, and societal attitudes will be crucial for achieving lasting change.

It is only through concerted effort and collaboration that we can pave the way for a future where every woman can exercise her rights freely and confidently, unburdened by the weight of historical injustices.

Topic 6

Wealth Management and Economic Disparities in Modern India

In the rapidly changing landscape of modern India, wealth management and economic disparities have become pressing issues that warrant thorough examination. As the nation embraces globalization and technological advancements, the economic landscape is transforming in ways that significantly affect the lives of its citizens. This topic explores the intricacies of wealth management in contemporary India, the widening economic divide, and the implications of these dynamics on various socio-economic groups. By delving into these themes, we can better understand how modernization has impacted wealth distribution and the challenges that arise from these changes.

Understanding Wealth Management

Defining Wealth Management

Wealth management refers to a comprehensive approach to managing an individual's or family's financial resources. This includes investment strategies, estate planning, tax management, and retirement planning. In India, the concept of wealth management has evolved considerably over the past few decades, largely due to economic liberalization and the emergence of a burgeoning middle class.

Wealth management is not limited to high-net-worth individuals; it increasingly extends to middle-income families seeking financial stability and growth. Financial literacy plays a crucial role in empowering individuals to make informed decisions about their money. However, despite this growing awareness, a significant portion of the population remains outside the purview of structured wealth management services.

The Growth of the Wealth Management Industry

The wealth management industry in India has witnessed substantial growth, driven by factors such as increased disposable income, rising entrepreneurship, and the proliferation of financial products. Numerous financial institutions, including banks, asset management companies, and independent advisors, have emerged to cater to the diverse needs of clients.

Despite this growth, the industry faces challenges related to accessibility and trust. Many individuals, especially from lower socio-economic backgrounds, lack access to quality financial advice and services. Additionally, the prevalence of mis-selling in the financial sector has led to a sense of skepticism among potential investors.

Economic Disparities in Modern India

The Widening Gap

As India progresses towards modernization, economic disparities have become increasingly pronounced.

The divide between the affluent and the underprivileged is stark, with a significant portion of the population struggling to meet basic needs while a small percentage accumulates immense wealth.

According to various reports, the wealthiest individuals in India possess a disproportionately large share of the country's wealth.

This concentration of wealth not only affects economic mobility but also impacts social dynamics, as disparities often lead to resentment and social unrest.

Impact on Different Socio-Economic Groups

The widening economic gap affects various socio-economic groups in distinct ways. For instance, the upper-middle class and affluent individuals often enjoy access to better education, healthcare, and employment opportunities, enabling them to accumulate more wealth.

In contrast, marginalized communities, especially those belonging to lower castes or tribal backgrounds, face systemic barriers that hinder their economic advancement.

Women, too, experience unique challenges in wealth accumulation. Traditional gender roles often limit women's access to education and employment opportunities, perpetuating cycles of poverty.

Even when women enter the workforce, they may encounter wage disparities and barriers to advancement.

The Role of Financial Literacy

Importance of Financial Literacy

Financial literacy is pivotal in navigating the complexities of wealth management and addressing economic disparities. A well-informed populace is better equipped to make sound financial decisions, invest wisely, and plan for the future.

In recent years, initiatives aimed at promoting financial literacy have gained traction. Schools, NGOs, and government programs have begun to incorporate financial education into their curricula, aiming to empower individuals from a young age. However, despite these efforts, a significant knowledge gap remains, particularly among rural populations.

Challenges in Promoting Financial Literacy

Several challenges impede the widespread adoption of financial literacy programs. Cultural attitudes toward money management, limited access to quality education, and language barriers can hinder the effectiveness of these initiatives. Additionally, many individuals may prioritize immediate financial needs over long-term planning, making it difficult to engage them in discussions about wealth management.

To address these challenges, tailored approaches that consider local contexts and cultural sensitivities are essential.

Community-based programs that leverage local resources and leaders can foster greater trust and engagement, ultimately promoting financial literacy in underserved areas.

The Impact of Modernization on Wealth Distribution

Globalization and Economic Opportunities

Globalization has played a significant role in reshaping India's economy. It has opened doors to new markets, increased foreign investments, and fostered entrepreneurship. However, the benefits of globalization have not been evenly distributed.

While urban areas have reaped the rewards of globalization, rural regions often lag behind. The disparity in access to resources, education, and infrastructure exacerbates existing inequalities, leaving many communities in poverty.

Additionally, the focus on high-tech industries and services can marginalize traditional sectors such as agriculture, further widening the economic divide.

Technological Advancements and Wealth Creation

The rise of technology has transformed wealth creation in India. Startups and tech-driven businesses have become prominent players in the economy, contributing to job creation and innovation. However, this shift has also led to a new form of economic disparity.

Individuals with access to technology and the skills to leverage it are often positioned to succeed, while those lacking such access face significant barriers. The digital divide is a critical issue, as rural areas frequently lack the infrastructure needed to benefit from technological advancements. Addressing this divide is crucial for ensuring that all citizens can participate in the modern economy.

Case Studies in Wealth Management

Urban vs. Rural Wealth Management

The approaches to wealth management vary significantly between urban and rural areas. In urban centers, financial institutions offer a plethora of services designed to cater to affluent clients, including sophisticated investment strategies and wealth planning.

Conversely, rural populations often lack access to formal financial services, relying instead on informal lending practices that can be exploitative.

A case study in a metropolitan city like Mumbai reveals how individuals leverage wealth management services to grow their assets. Conversely, in a rural village in Uttar Pradesh, families may struggle to access basic banking services, resulting in limited savings and investment opportunities.

This disparity underscores the need for inclusive financial solutions that bridge the gap between urban and rural wealth management practices.

Women and Wealth Management

Women's participation in wealth management has increased, yet they continue to face unique challenges. A case study focusing on women entrepreneurs in urban settings highlights how access to microfinance and mentorship programs has empowered women to start and grow their businesses.

However, women in rural areas often lack such opportunities, facing societal pressures that prioritize traditional roles over financial independence.

For instance, an analysis of women-led businesses in Bengaluru shows that with proper access to funding and resources, women can significantly contribute to economic growth.

However, this potential is often stifled in rural regions, where traditional norms and limited access to education hinder women's financial empowerment.

Government Policies and Initiatives

Role of Government in Wealth Distribution

The Indian government has implemented various policies aimed at addressing economic disparities and promoting inclusive growth. Initiatives such as the Pradhan Mantri Jan Dhan Yojana aim to increase financial inclusion by providing access to banking services for underserved populations.

However, the effectiveness of these programs often depends on local implementation and community engagement. To truly bridge the economic divide, policies must be tailored to address the unique challenges faced by different socio-economic groups.

Promoting Entrepreneurship

Encouraging entrepreneurship is another strategy the government employs to stimulate economic growth and reduce disparities. Programs that provide training, mentorship, and financial support to aspiring entrepreneurs can foster innovation and create jobs.

However, challenges such as bureaucratic hurdles, access to capital, and market competition can hinder entrepreneurial efforts, particularly among marginalized communities. Addressing these barriers is essential for ensuring that entrepreneurship becomes a viable pathway for economic advancement.

The Future of Wealth Management and Economic Equity

Creating Inclusive Financial Systems

To create a more equitable financial landscape, it is crucial to develop inclusive financial systems that cater to the diverse needs of the population.

This includes expanding access to financial education, offering tailored financial products, and promoting transparency in financial transactions.

Moreover, leveraging technology can play a transformative role in enhancing financial inclusion. Mobile banking and digital payment systems have the potential to reach underserved populations, providing them with the tools to manage their finances effectively.

Fostering Collaboration Between Sectors

Addressing wealth disparities and promoting effective wealth management requires collaboration between government, private sector, and civil society.

Partnerships that bring together various stakeholders can leverage resources, knowledge, and expertise to create comprehensive solutions.

For instance, collaborations between financial institutions and NGOs can facilitate financial literacy programs that reach marginalized communities.

Such partnerships can enhance the impact of initiatives aimed at promoting economic equity and financial empowerment.

In summary, wealth management and economic disparities in modern India reflect the broader challenges and opportunities presented by modernization.

While the growth of the wealth management industry and the rise of entrepreneurship signify progress, significant disparities persist, particularly between urban and rural populations, as well as among different socio-economic groups.

Addressing these disparities requires a multi-faceted approach that encompasses financial literacy, inclusive policies, and collaborative efforts across sectors.

By fostering an equitable financial landscape, India can work towards a future where all citizens have the opportunity to achieve financial stability and prosperity.

As the nation continues to navigate the complexities of modernization, it is essential to prioritize the well-being of all individuals, ensuring that economic growth benefits everyone, regardless of their background or circumstances.

Only through concerted efforts can we hope to bridge the economic divide and create a more just society for future generations.

Topic 7

Changes in Modern Relationships and Marriages in India

In the vibrant and diverse landscape of modern India, relationships and marriages are undergoing profound transformations influenced by globalization, technology, and evolving cultural norms. As societal expectations shift, the traditional frameworks that once defined love and partnership are being challenged and redefined.

This topic delves into the changing dynamics of modern relationships and marriages in India, exploring factors such as evolving gender roles, the impact of technology, new definitions of love and commitment, and the challenges these changes bring. By understanding these shifts, we gain valuable insights into how contemporary society navigates the complexities of love, commitment, and companionship.

Traditional Views on Relationships and Marriages

Historical Context

Traditionally, Indian marriages were largely arranged, with families playing a central role in matchmaking. These unions were seen more as alliances between families than as partnerships based on romantic love. Factors such as caste, religion, and socioeconomic status were paramount in determining compatibility. This system provided stability and social order but often left personal desires unaddressed.

Historically, the role of women in these arrangements was primarily that of caretakers and homemakers. Women were expected to conform to societal norms, often prioritizing family responsibilities over personal aspirations.

The ideal of the dutiful wife, committed to her family and children, was deeply ingrained in cultural narratives. In this context, love was frequently considered a secondary consideration, emerging only after marriage.

The Role of Family in Marriages

Family influence remains significant in the marriage process, though its nature is changing. While arranged marriages are still common, younger generations are increasingly seeking a balance between familial expectations and personal desires.

This has led to a growing acceptance of love marriages, wherein individuals choose their partners based on emotional connection rather than familial arrangement.

As societal norms evolve, many young couples now approach marriage with a desire for mutual compatibility and understanding. Families are beginning to adapt, recognizing that happiness in marriage is essential for the well-being of their children.

This shift signals a gradual transformation in how relationships are formed, emphasizing the importance of personal choice alongside familial consent.

Evolving Gender Roles

Changing Dynamics

The traditional gender roles that once defined relationships are undergoing significant transformation. Women are increasingly asserting their independence, pursuing higher education and careers, and challenging long-standing expectations.

This evolution is not confined to urban areas; even rural regions are witnessing gradual changes, albeit at a different pace. As women gain more agency, they are also reimagining their roles within relationships.

Conversely, men are navigating new expectations in the context of changing gender dynamics. The traditional notion of masculinity is evolving, with increasing emphasis on emotional intelligence, shared responsibilities, and active involvement in family life. This shift encourages men to embrace roles that prioritize nurturing and support, fostering more equitable partnerships.

Impact on Relationship Expectations

With the redefinition of gender roles comes a change in relationship expectations. Modern couples are more likely to seek companionship, mutual respect, and shared goals. The notion of partnership now encompasses emotional support, collaboration, and co-parenting. This expansion of what it means to be a partner allows for deeper connections and more fulfilling relationships.

Women, in particular, are looking for partners who respect their ambitions and values. As they gain financial independence, the desire for a partner who contributes equally and values their career aspirations becomes paramount. This shift prompts a reevaluation of what success looks like in relationships, moving beyond traditional gender expectations.

The Influence of Technology

Technology and Modern Dating

The advent of technology has revolutionized how people meet, interact, and form relationships. Online dating platforms and social media have broadened the horizons for connection, allowing individuals to explore potential partners beyond their immediate social circles.

Apps like Tinder and Bumble have gained immense popularity, particularly among younger generations, facilitating both casual dating and serious relationships.

While technology provides convenience and a wider pool of options, it also introduces challenges. The prevalence of "swiping culture" can lead to superficial interactions, where individuals prioritize physical attraction over deeper emotional connections.

The pressure to maintain an appealing online presence can distort perceptions of authenticity, making it challenging to cultivate genuine relationships.

Social Media's Impact on Relationships

Social media plays a complex role in modern relationships. On one hand, it serves as a platform for connection, enabling couples to share experiences and communicate seamlessly.

On the other hand, it can create unrealistic expectations and foster comparisons, leading to dissatisfaction and conflict. Couples may find themselves caught in a cycle of portraying an idealized relationship online while grappling with underlying issues in real life.

The challenge lies in balancing public and private personas. The pressure to showcase a perfect relationship on social media can strain real-life dynamics, leading to misunderstandings and insecurity.

Open communication becomes essential to navigating these challenges, as couples work to establish trust and authenticity in both their online and offline lives.

Redefining Love and Commitment

Changing Definitions of Love

The concept of love is undergoing a profound transformation in modern India. Traditionally, love was often viewed through the lens of duty and familial obligation.

However, contemporary relationships increasingly prioritize emotional intimacy and personal fulfillment. Young couples are more likely to seek partners who align with their values and aspirations, fostering connections built on shared interests and mutual respect.

Romantic love is gaining prominence, challenging the notion that love should develop after marriage. This shift has led to a rise in pre-marital relationships and cohabitation, which were once considered taboo.

The growing acceptance of these practices reflects a broader societal change, where individual desires are acknowledged alongside traditional expectations.

Commitment in the Modern Age

The concept of commitment is being redefined as well. Couples are exploring various forms of commitment, ranging from cohabitation without marriage to long-term partnerships that do not adhere to conventional timelines. This flexibility allows individuals to tailor their relationships according to their unique needs and circumstances.

Additionally, the increasing acceptance of non-traditional relationship structures, such as open relationships and polyamory, indicates a broader societal shift towards inclusivity and understanding.

This evolving landscape invites individuals to consider love and commitment in ways that reflect their authentic selves, moving beyond rigid definitions.

Challenges of Modern Relationships

Navigating Expectations

While modern relationships offer greater freedom and choice, they also come with unique challenges. The pressure to find the "perfect" partner can lead to unrealistic expectations and disappointment. Individuals may find themselves constantly comparing their relationships to those depicted online, resulting in feelings of inadequacy and dissatisfaction.

Moreover, balancing career aspirations with relationship commitments can be a daunting task. Many couples struggle to find the right equilibrium between personal goals and shared responsibilities, leading to stress and potential conflict. The challenge lies in recognizing that both partners must prioritize their individual dreams while also nurturing the relationship.

Dealing with Relationship Anxiety

The fear of commitment and relationship anxiety are increasingly prevalent in modern society. Past experiences, societal pressures, and personal insecurities can contribute to a reluctance to fully invest in a partnership.

Individuals may grapple with fears of vulnerability or an overwhelming desire to maintain independence at the expense of emotional intimacy.

Addressing these anxieties often requires open communication and a willingness to engage in therapeutic interventions. Couples who prioritize emotional honesty and seek professional guidance are better equipped to navigate the complexities of modern relationships. Building a foundation of trust and understanding is essential for overcoming these challenges.

The Impact of Cultural Changes

Cultural Shifts and Acceptance

As societal norms continue to evolve, there is a growing acceptance of diverse relationship structures. Conversations surrounding LGBTQ+ relationships, inter-caste marriages, and single parenthood are becoming increasingly mainstream.

This cultural shift reflects a broader recognition of the varied experiences and identities that exist within modern relationships.

Media representation plays a crucial role in shaping public perceptions. Films, television shows, and literature that portray diverse love stories can foster empathy and understanding, helping to dismantle stigma around non-traditional relationships.

As these narratives become more visible, society begins to embrace the idea that love can take many forms.

The Role of Education and Awareness

Education and awareness are essential in promoting healthy relationships. Programs that teach conflict resolution, communication skills, and emotional intelligence can empower individuals to build and maintain strong partnerships.

Schools and community organizations have a vital role to play in facilitating discussions about healthy relationships, encouraging young people to reflect on their values and aspirations.

By equipping individuals with the knowledge and tools to navigate relationships, we can foster a culture of respect and understanding. As younger generations learn to prioritize emotional well-being and communication, the likelihood of successful and fulfilling relationships increases.

The Future of Relationships and Marriages

Embracing Change

The future of relationships and marriages in India will likely continue to be shaped by ongoing social and cultural transformations. As individuals become more empowered to define their relationship choices, we can expect to see further diversification in how love and commitment are expressed. Couples may seek personalized approaches to marriage, focusing on what works best for them rather than adhering strictly to traditional norms.

This evolution may lead to the emergence of new rituals and practices that reflect the unique values and aspirations of couples. The emphasis on individual fulfillment will drive changes in how relationships are celebrated, prioritized, and nurtured.

Creating Supportive Environments

To foster healthy relationships, society must create supportive environments that encourage open dialogue and understanding. Families, communities, and institutions can work together to promote acceptance of diverse relationship choices, ultimately contributing to a more inclusive society.

As individuals navigate the complexities of modern love, access to resources such as counseling, workshops, and peer support becomes increasingly important.

By prioritizing emotional well-being and fostering connections based on mutual respect, we can pave the way for fulfilling and resilient relationships. Encouraging collaboration between partners and fostering environments where vulnerability is embraced can lead to deeper connections and a more compassionate understanding of love.

In conclusion, modern relationships and marriages in India are undergoing significant changes influenced by evolving gender roles, technological advancements, and shifting cultural norms.

While these changes present both opportunities and challenges, they ultimately reflect a broader societal shift towards individual empowerment and emotional fulfillment.

As we navigate this new landscape, it is essential to embrace the diversity of experiences and identities within relationships.

By promoting open communication, education, and acceptance, we can foster a society where all individuals have the freedom to define love and commitment on their own terms.

The journey toward understanding and embracing modern relationships is ongoing, and as India continues to evolve, so too will the dynamics of love and partnership.

It is an exciting time for individuals to explore new possibilities and forge connections that reflect their authentic selves, paving the way for a future where relationships are not only meaningful but also deeply fulfilling.

Conclusion

Reflections on the Future

As we take a moment to reflect on the intricate tapestry of modernization in India, it's clear that the landscape of relationships, cultural values, and social dynamics is undergoing a profound metamorphosis.

This transformation is not simply a clash of tradition and modernity; rather, it represents a complex dialogue that is actively reshaping the identities and aspirations of individuals across the nation.

One of the most striking findings from this exploration is the remarkable resilience of Indian society in adapting to new ideas while holding onto essential cultural values. Traditional concepts of family, marriage, and community are being redefined, creating a rich interplay between the past and the present.

For instance, while arranged marriages continue to be a significant aspect of Indian culture, there is an increasing acceptance of love marriages, cohabitation, and even non-traditional partnerships. This reflects a growing awareness of individual rights and desires, paving the way for a more nuanced understanding of what constitutes a successful partnership.

Moreover, the role of women in society is evolving dramatically. With increased access to education and career opportunities, women are asserting their independence in ways that challenge traditional gender roles.

They are not only becoming key decision-makers in their personal lives but are also emerging as influential figures in the broader socio-economic landscape. This shift is crucial for fostering a more equitable society and addressing longstanding gender disparities.

The impact of technology on relationships cannot be overstated. The rise of social media and dating apps has transformed the way individuals meet and connect. While these platforms offer unprecedented opportunities for interaction, they also introduce challenges such as superficial connections and the pressure to curate idealized online personas.

As individuals navigate these complexities, the ability to establish genuine emotional connections amidst a backdrop of digital noise becomes increasingly important.

Looking ahead, the future of modernization in India is poised for continued evolution. The younger generations are not only embracing change but actively seeking it. They are more likely to challenge societal norms, advocate for inclusivity, and explore diverse relationship structures.

As conversations around gender equality, LGBTQ+ rights, and mental health gain traction, society is gradually moving toward a more open and accepting paradigm.

However, this progress does not come without challenges. The growing pace of change can sometimes lead to tension between generations, with traditional values clashing against modern aspirations. Addressing these tensions will require empathy, dialogue, and a commitment to understanding differing perspectives.

As society navigates these complexities, it will be vital to foster environments where individuals feel safe to express their identities and relationships without fear of judgment or ostracism.

Call to Action

In light of these reflections, it is essential for readers to engage critically and constructively with the issues surrounding modernization in India. Here are several actionable steps to consider:

1. Educate Yourself and Others:

Delve into literature, documentaries, and discussions that challenge your viewpoints and expand your understanding of the multifaceted nature of modernization. Share insights within your communities to foster open dialogues and promote a culture of learning.

2. Advocate for Inclusivity:

Support organizations and initiatives that champion gender equality, LGBTQ+ rights, and the recognition of diverse family structures. Whether through volunteering, donations, or raising awareness, your involvement can contribute to meaningful change.

3. Reflect on Your Relationships:

Take the time to evaluate how the themes explored in this book resonate in your own life. Engage in open conversations with partners, friends, and family about your values, expectations, and aspirations, fostering deeper connections.

4. Participate in Community Dialogues:

Seek out workshops, seminars, and forums that focus on modern relationships, gender roles, and social change. Engaging with others who share similar interests can create a sense of community and collective learning, enriching the conversation.

5. Challenge Stereotype:

Be proactive in confronting and questioning stereotypes related to gender roles, relationships, and cultural expectations. Use your platform, whether it's social media, community groups, or workplace discussions, to advocate for change and promote a more inclusive narrative.

6. Practice Active Listening:

In conversations about relationships and societal change, practice active listening. Encourage others to share their experiences and perspectives, fostering a culture of empathy and understanding.

By engaging with these issues, we can collectively contribute to a more nuanced understanding of modernization in India and support the ongoing journey toward a more inclusive and equitable society.

Each of us has a role to play in this transformation, and together, we can create an environment where all individuals feel empowered to pursue their authentic selves.

Appendices

Resources for Further Reading

- Books:

  - "The Argumentative Indian" by Amartya Sen: A collection of essays that explore Indian culture, identity, and history, providing insights into the complexities of modern India.

  - "India: A History" by John Keay: A comprehensive account of India's rich history, offering context to contemporary issues and cultural shifts.

  - "Modern Love: Stories of Passion and Connection" edited by Daniel Jones: An anthology that examines love in all its forms, reflecting the changing nature of relationships in the modern world.

  - "Women and Indian Modernity" by Rina M. Nayak: A critical exploration of women's roles in contemporary India and the impact of modernization on their identities.

- Articles:

  - "The Changing Face of Marriage in India" (Harvard Business Review): An insightful analysis of the evolving nature of marriage and partnership in contemporary Indian society.

  - "Gender Roles in Modern Indian Society" (Journal of South Asian Studies): A scholarly examination of how gender dynamics are shifting within modern relationships.

  - "Technology and Relationships: A Study of Young Adults in India" (Indian Journal of Communication): Research that explores the impact of technology on the dating habits and relationship dynamics of young Indians.

- **Organizations**:

  - The Centre for Women's Development Studies (CWDS): An organization dedicated to research and advocacy for women's rights and gender equality in India.

  - Breakthrough India: An organization focused on using media and community engagement to address issues of gender inequality and promote social change.

  - The Alliance for Gender Equality: A collective that advocates for policies and practices supporting gender equality across various sectors.

Surveys and Studies

- **Data on Relationship Trends**:

A recent survey conducted by the Pew Research Center indicates that nearly 50% of young Indians prefer love marriages over arranged marriages, highlighting a significant cultural shift towards individual choice and autonomy in matters of love.

- **Impact of Technology**:

Research from the Indian Institute of Technology reveals that approximately 70% of urban youth engage with dating apps, illustrating the growing role of technology in shaping romantic relationships and social interactions.

- **Gender Roles**:

A study published in the Economic and Political Weekly found that 65% of men in urban areas support their partners' career ambitions, indicating a positive shift towards shared domestic responsibilities and a more equitable approach to gender roles.

References

- Sen, A. (2005). *The Argumentative Indian*. New York: Farrar, Straus and Giroux.

- Keay, J. (2000). *India: A History*. New York: HarperCollins.

- Nayak, R. M. (2018). *Women and Indian Modernity*. New Delhi: Sage Publications.

- Pew Research Center. (2020). *"The Changing Face of Marriage in India."*

- Indian Institute of Technology. (2021). *"Technology and Relationships: A Study of Young Adults in India."*

- Economic and Political Weekly. (2022). *"Gender Roles in Modern Indian Society."*